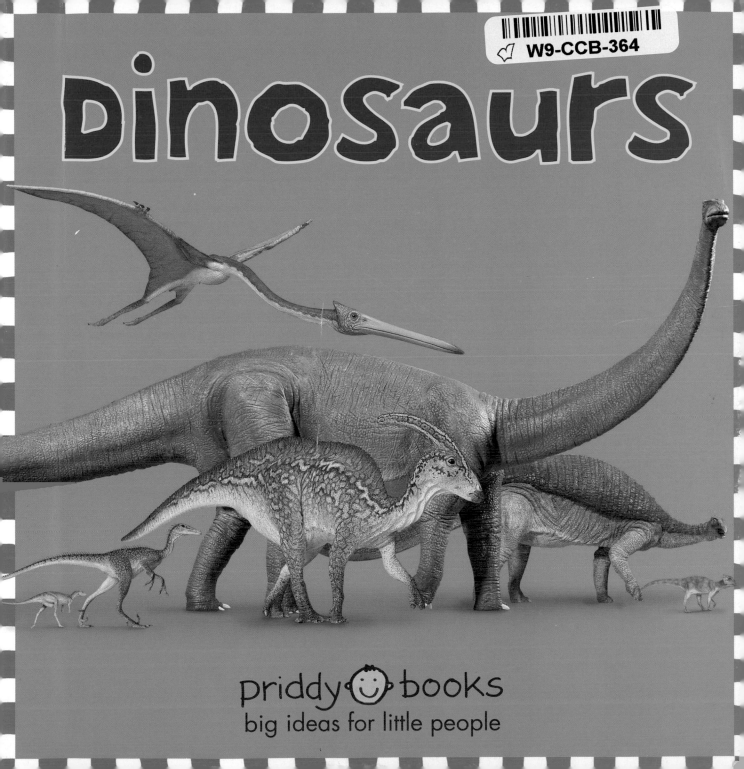

# Dinosaurs

priddy books
big ideas for little people

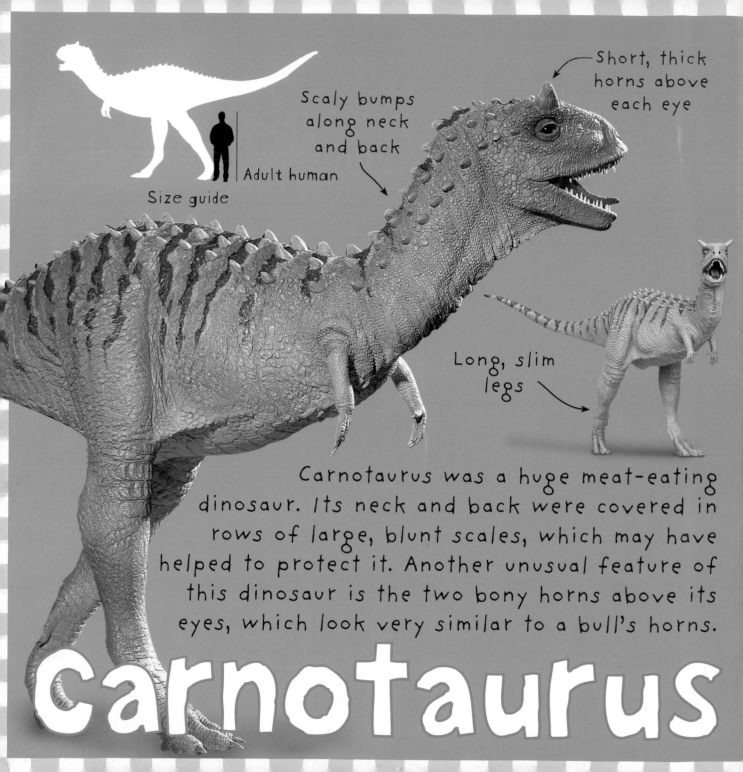

Scaly bumps
along neck
and back

Short, thick
horns above
each eye

Size guide

Adult human

Long, slim
legs

Carnotaurus was a huge meat-eating
dinosaur. Its neck and back were covered in
rows of large, blunt scales, which may have
helped to protect it. Another unusual feature of
this dinosaur is the two bony horns above its
eyes, which look very similar to a bull's horns.

# Carnotaurus

# Baryonyx

Size guide

Baryonyx is one of the only dinosaurs known to have eaten fish. It may have caught this slippery prey using the large, hook-like claws on its thumbs. Discovered in the south of England, the name Baryonyx also means "heavy claw."

Narrow crocodile-like, jaws

Strong claws for catching fish

Euoplocephalus was a heavily armored plant-eater. It had very thick skin, covered in bony plates. This slow-mover's most impressive protection was its bony tail club, which it swung at attackers.

Heavy club on end of tail

# Euoplocephalus

Large, bony spikes protect the head and neck

Size guide

Gravitholus was a plant-eater with a very unusual head. There were extra-thick bones on the top of its skull, which is why it is sometimes called a "bonehead." These dinosaurs may have pushed into enemies' sides as defense, or charged at male rivals.

Size guide

Thick, dome-shaped skull

Long, slim legs and feet helped it to run quickly

# Gravitholus

Sharp claws

Very long, thin neck

Coelophysis was a small, fast dinosaur. It had very hollow bones, making it lightweight and able to travel quickly. This helped it to catch prey and escape enemies.

Size guide

# Coelophysis

# Diplodocus

Small head

45-foot long, whip-like tail

26-foot long neck

Size guide

Large claw on toe of each foot

Diplodocus was one of the longest dinosaurs that ever lived, and could grow to the length of a tennis court. This plant-eater digested food by swallowing stones that then mashed up plants in its stomach.

# Janenschia

Long neck helped it to eat plants from trees

Janenschia was one of the sauropods— a group of plant-eaters that were the largest animals to have ever lived. This enormous dinosaur was more than 80 feet long, and had a huge appetite. It could stand upright on its back legs, reaching to eat from tall trees.

Size guide

Bony plates

Very strong legs support its weight

# Iguanodon

Size guide

Wide,
toothless beak

Sharp thumb
spike

Iguanodon was one of the most
commonly found dinosaurs. It had
five-fingered hands with an unusual
bony spike on the thumb. This may have
been used to collect food, or for protection.

Beak-like
mouth

Flexible
neck

Hadrosaurus was part of a group
of plant-eaters called "duckbills."
They were named after the unusual
shape of their mouths. Their beaks were
toothless, but in the back of their mouths there
were as many as 2,000 teeth to chew up food.

# Hadrosaurus

# Stegosaurus

Tail
spikes

Biggest
plates up to
2 feet wide →

Size guide

Stegosaurus is a very well-recognized dinosaur. Thin, bony plates covered its neck, back, and tail, and it had at least four sharp spikes on the end of its tail. This spiky tail was its main defense, and when it lashed out at attackers, it could cause a nasty injury.

# Tyrannosaurus rex

Bony ridges on top of the head

Tyrannosaurus rex was a huge, fearsome meat-eater with an enormous head. Its strong, muscular jaws were filled with hundreds of razor-sharp teeth. Some experts even think its mouth was big enough to swallow a person whole!

Size guide

Small arms

Size guide

Zephyrosaurus was a small, speedy dinosaur that just ate plants. Traveling in herds, it moved on two legs using its long, stiff tail to help with balance. Its body was designed for running quickly in order to escape danger.

Strong jaws to chew plants quickly

Five-fingered hands

Very long back legs

# Zephyrosaurus

# Parasaurolophus

Long, hollow
head crest

Thick,
padded
feet

Knobbly skin

Size guide

Parasaurolophus was a duckbill
relative of Hadrosaurus. It had an
unusual, hollow head crest with a
distinctive tube shape. This may have been
used to recognize others in its herd, or to make
loud sounds. Males had larger crests than females.

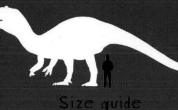
Size guide

Long,
heavy tail

# Allosaurus

Allosaurus was a large, fearsome meat-eater that may have hunted in packs. This dinosaur is thought to have been a very brutal predator. As well as sharp teeth and claws, it probably used its arms to grab a hold of its victims. It may have also stunned its prey with its long tail.

Powerful jaws

Clawed feet

6-inch long claws

Sharp spikes along the neck

Long, thin jaw

Size guide

Long, sickle-like claw on second toe

Bird-like Troodon is thought to have been one of the most intelligent dinosaurs. Its relatively large brain and big eyes could have helped it find prey more easily and hunt at night. It probably ate small reptiles or mammals.

# Troodon

Two long horns
up to 3 feet long

Size guide

Sharp beak
to cut up
plants

# Triceratops

Triceratops was a big, three-horned
vegetarian. It had an enormous head with a
solid bone neck frill. This dinosaur looked very
like a modern-day rhinoceros, and may have
charged at enemies or rivals in a similar way.

Brachiosaurus was one of the largest sauropods, and more than twice the size of a giraffe. This giant vegetarian had a bony head crest, which is where its nostrils were. It stood upright, and had unusually long front legs compared to its back ones.

# Brachiosaurus

30-foot long neck to reach up high

Nostrils on top of its head

Large, flat teeth

Size guide

# Velociraptor

Size guide

Long, flat snout

Sharp, curved teeth

Velociraptor was a small but vicious killer. It had a long, retractable claw on the middle toe of each foot, and curved claws on its hands. It was also very fast, and may have chased its prey at speeds of up to 40 miles an hour.

Sharp claw

# Quetzalcoatlus

10-foot long neck

This large, flying reptile lived around the same time as the dinosaurs, and was the biggest creature ever to fly. With huge wings made of leathery skin, meat-eating Quetzalcoatlus would swoop down and catch its prey using its pointed beak.

18-foot long wings

Size guide

Three sharp, claw-like fingers